MW00627550

Storms can deter us from living our potential. They often can come with scars and voices that we try to conceal. MariLynn reveals what she has uncovered in her journey of healing so that you may conquer storms, illuminate scars, and proclaim your voice.

—Jody Almond
Pastor, CEO of Soulution Ministries
#1 Amazon best selling author of
Going All In- Finding Success Through Surrender

Check Yourself Out is a journey of empowerment and acceptance through healing. MariLynn's perseverance shines through as she reveals how storms can be conquered and voices manifested to living fully and authentically.

—Melody Lee
Mindset & Breakthrough Coach

I highly recommend Check Yourself Out because it really captures the heart of the writer. It allows you to look into her world from many lenses. The form of the book isn't anything I have seen before, but real Art work comes from those who dare to be different! It's a relatable and fantastic read!

—Andrew S. Oakes
Expert Stress Coach and Motivational Speaker

Storms can discourage and prevent us from fully living. In MariLynn's journey, she reveals perseverance and guidance so that you may breakthrough the storms and proclaim your voice.

—Michael Barata
Life Coach

CHECK YOURSELF OUT

Magnify Your Voice and Manifest Your Authentic Life to Conquer Inner Storms

MariLynn Bolton

Check Yourself Out © 2021 by MariLynn Bolton. All rights reserved.

Published by Author Academy Elite
PO Box 43, Powell, OH 43065
www.AuthorAcademyElite.com

All rights reserved. This book contains material protected under international and federal copyright laws and treaties. Any unauthorized reprint or use of this material is prohibited. No part of this book may be reproduced or transmitted in any form or by any means, electronic or mechanical, including photocopying, recording, or by any information storage and retrieval system, without express written permission from the author.

Identifiers:
LCCN: 2021920327
ISBN: 978-1-64746-937-5(paperback)
ISBN: 978-1-64746-938-2(hardback)
ISBN: 978-1-64746-939-9(ebook)

Available in paperback, hardback, e-book, and audiobook

Any Internet addresses (websites, blogs, etc.) and telephone numbers printed in this book are offered as a resource. They are not intended in any way to be or imply an endorsement by Author Academy Elite, nor does Author Academy Elite vouch for the content of these sites and numbers for the life of this book.

The stories and my journey in this book are mine alone. This is what has worked for me. It is not meant to replace the advice of a doctor or any professional help. The flower and leaf illustrations are also my own drawings during my journey. The book and feather illustration is from WordArt.

DEDICATION

From the creators, guardians, angels, and dreamers to the weary and timid souls, this book is dedicated to you. I know we haven't met but I do know you are the light of hope and love.

For my husband, Cliff, my daughters, Ashley, Kalee, and Riley, and grandchildren, Chloe, Justin Jr., and Jude: You have supported and believed in me. Your songs, smiles, laughter, and hugs have given me everlasting strength and love.

TO THE READER

Life is full of beautiful days of sunshine, clear skies, and engulfing fierce storms. It can be difficult to find the balance when storms seem to last longer than what we want them to. Inner storms can be the toughest and most complex to combat.

Certain mindsets and beliefs that worked in the past may not work for our future. We overflow and blend into each others' journeys. There is balance, distaste, bitterness, hunger, and more. When we look beyond the mirror at the reflection, relationships, and our trials and triumphs, then we can become the best version of ourselves, whatever that means in each stage of our lives.

As we learn to listen and engage in conversations with ourselves rather than over thinking, then doubts and negative thoughts can be tamed. It's not easy. It can be yucky, squirmy, and downright awkward; with every making of a masterpiece, there are remnants, chaos, disorder, and clutter. We are constantly evolving into who we are meant to be.

When you are tired, take time out to rest, heal, and gain inner strength with a new perspective. After all, it's a new day and this new day needs you. May you find comfort and courage in your journey. May you discover parts of your self that have been yearning to be seen and heard. May you be inspired to shine in your truth.

You are loved. You make a difference. You are not alone. I survived—no, I conquered the fiercest and deadliest of storms that has ever come my way and so can you. I believe in you.

CONTENTS

INTRODUCTION

Fear, anxiety, and depression became a part of my life. Many times, I felt the sting of rejection, loneliness, abandonment, and like I wasn't enough for anyone. I learned to hide my emotions so I didn't get hurt. I didn't know how to talk about my pain. Happiness seemed to be the only acceptable emotion to show. The happy face was molding perfectly, the music was numbing the pain, and I poured out my soul onto vacant pages. Day by day, it was getting easier to wear that mask and hide my soul. I became exactly how some people wanted to see me. I wore that mask for many years.

I have been one of the many unseen, unheard, and misunderstood souls. There was hiding, craving, loneliness, and fear. I didn't want to feel that way anymore and didn't want anyone else to feel that way.

It is our responsibility to educate ourselves about how to talk about both physical and mental health. We are more than labels on the inside and outside. We are strong and caring souls. With education, compassion, empathy, and love, we can tear off labels to accept and embrace each other through our sunshine and storms.

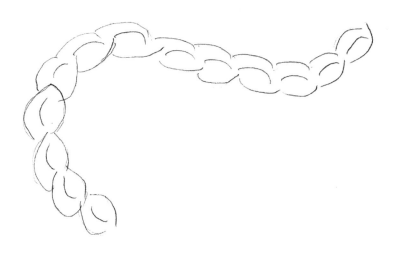

ELEPHANTS

In the corner or against the wall,
It wants to talk and at times seems small.
It always has so much to say. Jumps around
In everyone's way. It starts as one then comes in
Herds all because of the unspoken words. It eats away at the
Peace rapidly growing morbid obese. By calmly expressing our
Feelings inside it becomes weaker
And dissatisfied. No more slithering
Around with gloom.
It's time to get rid
Of the elephant
In the room.

CHAPTER 1
PROCEED WITH CAUTION

Whether the skies show sunshine or a chance of rain, I strive to start and keep a positive attitude. Brisk winds challenge me at times as I push through. Sleep is pushed aside so I can stay up late to help with my children's' school projects, watch a movie with my husband, or work extra hours.

TIME OUT

Time
Out
Isn't
A child
Thing.

Everyone needs a
Time out. Think before
You speak. Those few
Seconds of thinking
Make a world of
Difference. It can make
The eyes sparkle, A
Hug bigger, love stronger.
It can make someone's
Day brighter to take time out
By sharing the best of you.

STARS IN YOUR EYES

"Ok,
Child
Let's have
Some fun. Find the
First star. Make a wish." I give
You a hug and a forehead kiss. We look at the
Stars sparkling light. I see your smile shining bright. We play
The game of shapes to be found. We get dizzy
as we spin around. Countless stars
Have come out to play. This moment at night
has completed our day. "One in
A million stars in the skies. My favorite is the ones in your eyes."
The stars relate to life from this simple view: We shine
From the light in others. "My dear child,
I love you." Forever
And always
I love
You.

It seemed like just when I had learned how to balance life's' questions, then the answers changed. Learning to adjust to changes is a part of life.

CHANGING TIMES

Clouds roll in and skies darken.
Navigating through life's storms has plenty of challenges.
We watch, listen, and proceed with caution.

The sun is blazing hot today but it feels like I'm in a fog. This daily headache is pushing on my eyes and I can't seem to push through this. Getting glasses has mildly helped. Something still doesn't feel right because the fogginess hasn't gone away. *What is wrong with me?* I'm searching for answers again.

I wonder if it was something I ate or didn't eat or if I'm drinking enough water. I read somewhere that caffeine is known to help headaches. Maybe an extra shot or two of espresso will stop the pain. I'm pushing through to give all that I've got, but it doesn't seem to be enough. In fact, I am not enough for some and too much for others.

FIRST SIP

First sip of
Adrenaline
Rush from the
Comfort liquid of
The morning routine
Gives me confidence
To clear the fog away.
First sip is a trap.
Second sip entices,
Heightens the
Craving of the
Fog clearing.
Insides drenched
With temporary
Satisfaction.

I'm tired of all the advice!

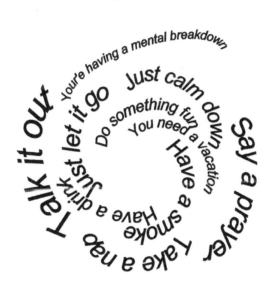

I just want the pain to stop!
I am becoming numb to the downpour advice as the pain settles in.

TIRED OF BEING TIRED

Layers of tread marks
Among dirt and worms,
Tangled in weeds.
Eyes no longer
Wandering side to side.
I'm somewhere
In the middle of nowhere
Tired of being tired.

The pain lurks around, teasing me with temporary spurts of relief. I want to scream—no sound comes out. I want to cry—I'm dried up. I'm in a fog of nothing—my memory is escaping. *When did I eat last? Where am I supposed to be? How did I get here? What is their name? Forgetting is normal, right?*

Speech is slurred, vision is blurred, balance is unstable, and the left side of my face feels like its being yanked off. Pain is excruciating and brain fog is haunting. Emergency room, here I come. Test result rule out many things, and they send me home. Three days of medicated sleep have left me exhausted. It will take time, but I will recover and gain my strength.

It didn't take long to go from an appointment with my doctor to a neurologist to be diagnosed with migraines. I start a routine of medications and go back to work. I know it will be trial and error to see what medications will work for me.

After a couple weeks, I try a new medication. This weekend is foggier and slower than usual. Not feeling my best is becoming the norm and more unsettling. By Monday morning at work, a co-worker catches me as I vigorously shake and fall to the ground. Words temporarily escape me. My slurred speech returns so my coworkers talk to my husband. He rushes to me. Luckily, it's only a few minutes' drive to the doctor. The seizure-like episodes continue during the drive there, in the waiting room, and in the patient room. Immediately, they take me off the new medicine. Work is on hold until the doctors can stabilize and clear me, so to help with the pain, they felt the best method was to give me muscle relaxers and pain killers, which put me into medicated sleep. The diagnosis is now chronic migraines.

DOWNPOUR

No end in sight of this storm
That has left a mess in my path.
It tries to drown out
The rest of the world
As if to take center stage.

"I see you.
I hear you.
Please hurry along your way."

The winds devour my words
As I shout to the skies.

The muscle relaxers and pain killers doctors prescribed help to stabilize me. Thunder and lightening shake the fog and pierce through the calm as the medicine wears off.

CHAPTER 2
HIDE AWAY

Bedridden and medicated is not stopping the cruel course of pain. Tears cascade down my cheeks in silence.

Stay calm. Breathe in. Breathe out.

I'm yearning for the cocktail pills to settle in. Loved ones take turns holding me and turn on comforting music as I drift off to sleep. The rhythm of old and new memories is soothing music for my soul.

Finally, some relief from pain, yet the abrupt absence of music is startling.

Memories of loneliness and abandonment collide, reminding my why I learned not to cry or show pain. I learned to show happiness, because to show anything else meant I was weak. I learned to build walls to protect myself so I didn't get hurt. It didn't matter anyway. No one asked me how I felt.

FORGOTTEN ONE

I've learned to hold the pillow tight.
No more tears getting me through the night.
I've learned how to not care
By gazing at the blank stare.
For every stranger that I see
Is a silent nightmare to me.
I hear screams vanish in the air.
Nothing left to give.
Nothing left to dare.
Emptiness has become
My nightmare, my daydream.
I live in silence with the title of
The Forgotten One.

Depression and anxiety welcome me to stay a while. *Why are they back? Did they not learn? Did I not learn?* They have held me down in the past and are up to their old tricks. I am surrounded by old acquaintances that accept me. *Is this where I belong?*

A LOST SOUL

Pleasing others,
Losing in
Amusing others,
Temporary fix
For the darkness.
Missing the piece
For self delight,
Timid flame
Deep inside.
No one sees
The lonely and sad
Soul hurting.

I'm tired of all the advice!

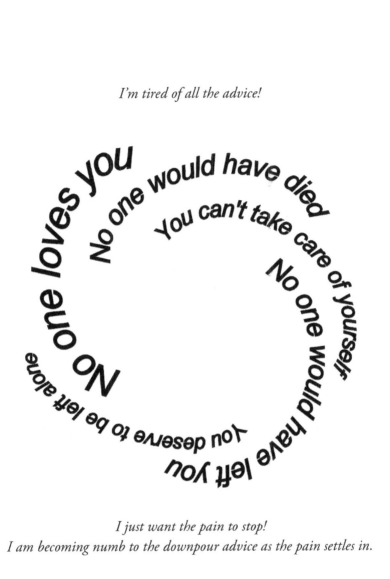

I just want the pain to stop!
I am becoming numb to the downpour advice as the pain settles in.

MIXED REMARKS

One more remark towards destruction.
The multitude of mixed remarks is convincing.
I believe every doubt in the spiral thread of lies.

I'm done defending myself. I'm done inviting anyone to see the real me.

INFUSING

One layer of truth
Is shredded to make room
For a layer of fakeness.
Left alone figuring
Out what mask fits each occasion.
The mask infuses
Molding another layer of skin.

Today, I stay off medication to stay awake and alert. There is peace and comfort as I spend a few hours with family. Months of different specialists and tests leave me with mixed answers. Nothing wrong here; nothing wrong there. Results do not match the pain I'm going through.

OXYGEN REPLACED

I'm crying out for answers
Feeling painted with despair.
Depression is replacing
The oxygen in the air.

The medication has taken away my pain and put my life on hold. The diagnosis is now debilitating complex chronic migraines.

FOSSIL

Running
Next to the brick wall.
Grasping at the bricks hoping
For support to pull myself forward.
Each step is cement-filled shoes. An invisible
Choker takes my breath away while allowing
My eyes to be the only thing I have control over.
No feeling of the tears dripping off my cheeks.
My hands don't hurt like the wall shows
They should. What have I become?
Another painting on the wall. A
Pebble on the path.
A petrified specimen
Could be
An
Improvement.

I have accepted I have to be dependent on others. After all, I have memory loss, can rarely form words, and I can't walk on my own. *What can I do for myself?* It feels like a switch in my brain shut off. This is my life now.

A SOLO WAR

Each day I add a layer
To make thicker walls and
Line the doorway
With a new lock.
Nothing can break through now.

Strangers unwelcome.
Stay away!
Nothing to see, Trespasser!
The locks are on fire!
Leave me to burn!

Another layer written
From the inside.

Goodbye!
I've been fighting myself; fighting for myself

A solo war.

CHAPTER 3

I CARE

My family helps me to walk around the house for some exercise. They hold my drink as I sip from a straw and help feed me. That is tiring. It is time to go back to bed. They adjust my pillow, tuck me in, and turn on the soft music.

Once again, the music stops. This is the shelter full of love, giving, and protection.

I try to protect others the only way I know how.

I TAKE THE HITS

I am your safe place.
I am your punching bag.
I take the hits.
I'm protecting myself
While you let out your anger.
When the tears roll down
From exhaustion,
You melt into my arms.

Forget boundaries, I wanted to be everything to everyone and do whatever it took to help others, to see others happy. I didn't know when or how to say no. I didn't know what it would cost.

WHIRL WIND

I didn't abandon you
When things seemed the darkest
For you. The darkness was becoming
A whirl wind sucking you in.
I'm on the other side
Trying to keep the
Light shining
For you to
Let you know
You don't
Have stay
There in the dark.

The chilling carnage of others' trauma crash into mine.

HEAVY LOAD

I will carry your burdens along with mine.
I will bury my anguish to help you shine.
I will be by your side until they are lighter.
The day will come when life is much brighter.
One more day is better than the last.
Live for the present and let go of the past.
Stay true to yourself and remember your goal.
Be proud of each step towards being whole.

I sacrificed every part of me for others. It came at a cost of bondage and self-destruction.

I CARE ABOUT YOU

I care about you
But I can't carry you.
The burdens that I carry
Not all of them are mine.
I'm not angry.
I'm not hurt.
I'm not even disappointed.
Not anymore.
I separate myself
From other's decisions
I willingly have taken
On as my own
Emotional battle to carry.
I do not own it.
I never have.

SAVING

I can't save you unless you let go.
I can't save myself if I don't let go.

MAYBE

Maybe it's meant to be:

The best thing you have ever had.

Only for a little while.

Guiding you for something new.

Maybe it's time to be let go.

CHAPTER 4

MASQUERADE HOUSE

Walls can keep people out or keep people in. The past is giving me a tour of what I tried to forget.

It is not easy letting people in, to let them get close to me. People think they know me.

PAPER THIN

You might think the paper walls are thin
Or you that you could walk through them with a grin.
You might think it easy. To me it is a sin
To make my walls crumble from a break in.

LAYER UPON LAYER

You have been invited several times before.
You act as if you were assigned a terrible chore.
I add a layer on my wall and add a lock on the door.
I'll stop asking you to come in. I don't want a war.
Layer upon layer unresponsive I've become.
All the words from you have made me numb.
Go back to where you came from.
You are not welcome.

Why can't I break free from these petrifying storms? I built these walls thick and strong to protect me.

BUILDING MY WALLS

I built up a wall
To protect myself
From negativity
That arises in life.
I built the wall
so others didn't get hurt
While still trying to shine my light.
Yet here I stand alone
No windows or doors
For most of the world anymore.
There is powerful limited light
I allow in.
Not completely giving in
To break down the walls,
To leave myself vulnerable.
It has taken time
To build these walls
Of overwhelming protection.
I've made them resistant
To outside sources.
Or so I thought.

Deeper into the silent abyss is where disconnected shadows roam free and secrets are concealed. This is where the elephants live.

ARRIVAL

After the elephants,
The abundance of silence
Becomes the invitation
For demons to arrive.

My protection, security, shield, defensive, everything I am is within these walls. The walls I have built to protect myself have become my prison.

SECRETS OF THE DARKNESS

Flames get bigger.
Secrets of the darkness
Now belong to me.
Dance with the Devil
In the flame light.
Smoke filled days.

Through the smog, I stumble to the bathroom on my own and grab onto the counter. An untamed numbing beast stares back at me. *What is this distorted figure?*

THE BEAST

Screams are in the air with sounds I do not know.
Shrieking runs down my back. Wish far away it would go.
Pounding sounds of anguish. Can't this monster be tamed?
Clouds of fury engulf me. Who wears the crown of shame?
The daggered words slash away at everything in sight.
Hatred boils over drowning everything for spite.
This battle is over. The air is becoming clearer.
The one who wears the crown is revealed in the mirror.

Is that really me?
What have I become?

I wish to look away yet I have become numb.
I stare into the blood shot eyes of the monster I have unleashed.
It seems there is one thing to make It complete.
A name so grand to put tears in your eyes.
Anyone who chooses to anger the beast is unwise.
It's only fair to warn you of the beast behind these eyes.
It is my magic crown. Above all else I will rise!
I control this beast of mine appearing as I need
To burn anything in Its path.

I will succeed!
I will have order!
I demand respect!
I wear the crown!
Don't you forget!

How can anyone love something so hideous?

I stumble back to bed, letting the shadows lull me back to sleep.

CHAPTER 5

GUARDIANS

SILENT SCREAMS

Silent screams in the night
It puts her heart to shame.
Did he hear? Can he feel?
Here comes the change again.
She knows he sees her sinking
He will not let her drown.
He smiles at her, holds her hand
While she wears a frown.
In her mind she wonders
Why is he still there?
Why doesn't he go away?
Does he truly care?
She's traveling on the road
That leads to the brink.
He sits by her side
With her favorite drink.
He smiles at a blank face.
She appears to be numb.
Is it becoming too much
For either to overcome?

BODYGUARD

She's got leaving on her mind.
She begins to fade away.
It is about that time.
Yet her body is here to stay.
He reaches out and hopes she smiles.
He wants to set her free.
The wall is up. The door is locked.
He doesn't have the key.
He checks on her through the window.
Is it driving him insane?
Is he lonely and empty?
Can he feel her pain?
He doesn't know where she goes
When she's got leaving on her mind.
He becomes her bodyguard.
That's what the universe designed.

MY ANGEL

I'm in such a hurry
Always making days rush by.
I say I will be alright. It's time to spread my wings and fly.
A stack of things to do. Loads of work undone. I have to go faster.
I'm always on the run. I have to keep going.
I can't seem to stop at all. Here
Comes the headache from meeting the brick
wall. I overdo it once again trying to do
Far too many things. I have to keep grounded.
I'm not the one with wings.

Why can't I get a break?
Listen
Where do I go from here?
Listen
When will my heart stop hurting?
Listen
My angel keeps whispering in my ear.
Listen

Calmness surrounds me as my tears are wiped away
"Time to rest. Gain your strength. Get ready for another day."
I willingly surrender. I am ready for sleep. My angel is holding me
And softly weeps. My angel cried for me
today and took away some pains.
I was guarded by the wings of love and heard no complaints.
My angel watches over me
Even times when I stray.
Not often enough do I imagine
Angels stopping to pray.

The fog begins to fade, as daily routines become my life-saver.

HOLD ME

Hold
Me
When
I
Fall
Down.
Let me cry
In your arms.
Hug me long
Enough allowing your
Strength to give me power.
Talk to me about little things,
For those are the big things
That matter. Let me get a glimpse
Of you looking at me with a grin, a
Wink or any gesture showing me you
Care. When I'm ready to talk be gentle
With your words. As you build me up my
Defensives will go down. Weakness will
Soon be in the past. I will be stronger,
Powerful, and resilient as my fears
Fade. My dimmed light is once again
Becoming a fireball of passion
From compassion and love.

My right hand is the only thing I seem to have some control over. *Straw, eat, drink,* and *I love you* are some of the things I learn in sign language. I ask for some paper and a pencil. I draw a line then another one and so on. This is what I have so I will do something.

SOUNDS OF THE BEAST

The words of the beast echo.
How can it be those words came from me?
I take a deep breath and remove the distorted band.
I blow away the pieces that have crumbled in my hands.
No longer does a beast dictate my fate.
Flames of love and laughter cannot wait.
This candle of flames inside of me
Is what I choose for the world to see.

CHAPTER 6
RELEASE

Disabled and memory loss, so they say. Well, through the dissipating fog, I remember who I use to be. Bursts of light remind me what I have accomplished and conquered.

I remember who I am.

GRAND CREATION

I look around inspecting what I built to protect myself.
No one needs to see my scars that are built into these walls.
I pull myself up and step away
From my emotionless comfort
Allowing some light to shine through.
I stumble through the mundane routines in life.
I raise the walls higher hoping no one sees.
It took time to master protecting myself,
To make these enormous walls sturdy.
I never imagined that I had the ability to create
Something so grand and powerful!
I never imagined how cold I would be.
I thought I was loving myself but I've been burying myself.
If my demons believe in me then so can I!

But I've been burying myself.
If my demons
Believe in me then so can I!

Labels will not stop me. The past does not define me or my future.

I HAVE ANXIETY

I have anxiety.
Anxiety does not have me.
It likes to slither in an undesirable gift
At the most inconvenient times.
A camouflage of eloquent beauty
Of lies opens a panic attack.
Releasing a deep breath
Creates a smile deep within me
Forcing anxiety to be dormant once more.
Descending tears of victory
Over anxiety prevails once again.

My over thinking skills left me with the conclusion that advice such as "Just calm down" is like having anxiety showing up on Valentine's Day with fruitcake.

I have learned to accept anxiety and that it can be helpful as long as I don't give it my power.

SEVERED SERVICES

Gather round my demons, I want to thank you all.
Each with unique traits you share with me.
Anxiety, fear, anger, and doubts just to name a few,
Thank you for believing in me.
For all the things you do,
The best has been
You showing me
What I can be.
How strong you
Can become
To overtake my sanity,
Leading me to the edge
To drown myself in your wisdom and power.
Piece by piece, I recreate your techniques
To be a master among masters.

I release you of your services.

CHAPTER 7

MASTERPIECE

MUDDLE THROUGH THE

PUDDLES

I'll muddle through the
Puddles while looking through
The rain one step at a time. Maybe one
Day the thunder and lightning will roll on by
Clouds will be dry and it will be my time to chase the
Rainbow. Until then, may the wind be at my back and
Worries washed away. May the waves gently calm my
Heart. May my hands reach out to others as others
Have reached out to me. I will not wait for the
Storm to cease. I will catch the rainbow
That is inside of me.

My body is weak, but my soul is stronger. I will dominate the storms, the fires, the battles, whatever comes my way. There are still some things that I cannot do for now. I am stronger than yesterday. I will be stronger tomorrow.

CHECK YOURSELF OUT

Check yourself out. Break from the mold.
Tear off the label before your heart grows old.
Give yourself credit for all that you do.
Challenge yourself to learn something new.
Inspire!
Enlighten!
Empower!
Break through!
Let your soul shine to show the real you.
You can stand alone or with a crowd.
Whatever you do, be strong and be proud.
It's time to check yourself out!

BELIEVE

Be connected not bound.
Be a voice not a sound.
Wear a smile on your face.
Give a hug full of embrace.
Look yourself in the eye.
Believe now is the time to try.

Another sketch book is filled up and it's time for another one. I've captured beauty in black and white but today I add blue and pink. A hidden talent I didn't know I had.

What else can I do?

MAYBE TOMORROW

Today is the day to conquer the world!
Maybe Tomorrow.
I'm going to move mountains!
-piles of laundry
Maybe Tomorrow.
It's a mountain of many colors!
I repeat: Maybe Tomorrow.
-stack of dishes will crash!
Maybe Tomorrow.
Time for a magic trick, Jenga, Jenga, Jenga®
I repeat: Maybe Tomorrow.

I proclaim this land the home of missing socks, Tupperware®,
Last minute assignments, and array of colorful mounds around.
The Land of Make-Believe.
No time to rest. No time to be sick. No time for myself.
Maybe Tomorrow.
Hey, Cinderella! Can I borrow your Fairy Godmother, please!?
Maybe Tomorrow.
Today I will conquer the world
One mountain at a time.
One prayer at a time.
Maybe Tomorrow needs a prayer today.

CREATE SOMETHING

Everyday we create something
We create meals, messes, smiles, and moods.
We are more than what we think we already know about ourselves.

WEIGHING DOWN

The past has been weighing down my future.
A new day is before me.
I choose what layers
To continue living with.
I have to let some go.
They don't fit anymore.

A NEW DAY

Today is a new day.
Your strength today
Is not measured
By strength yesterday.
Each day requires
Different levels of strength.
Go easy on yourself.
You got this.

Walking ten steps feels lighter today. I drag a chair into the bathroom and pad it with pillows. After brushing my hair, I dab on yellow and green eye shadow to brighten my eyes. I'll try different colors another day.

CELEBRATE

Accept weaknesses and strengths.
Celebrate both.
In trying to hide or dismiss either one
We ultimately lose ourselves.
Recognize and accept them.
Self-empowerment comes easier
With self-awareness and self-control.
This is who I am.
No explanations. No excuses.
I celebrate all of me.

Every step I choose is up to me and today I choose to rest. Resting is essential for strength and progress. I will celebrate every moment.

THE ONLY WAY TO BE

I know who I am.
I know I am strong.
I believe in myself.
I need to remind myself,
Teach myself this
Is the only way to be.
Then and only then will
The doubts be blocked.
Only then, with my own
Strength, do I allow the best
Of me by your side. The strength
Of us as one gives more light and power to shine.

ILLUMINATES

Another scar illuminates
Joining the multitude,
Creating the masterpiece of me.

I WOKE UP TODAY

I stretch the aching bones this morn' as I start waking up in bed.
I say a little prayer after shaking the cobwebs from my head.

Dear Lord,
Thanks for letting me wake up today.
There is pain in my back. My left arm fell asleep.
I hear the dog bark and the loud alarm beep.

Dear Lord,
Thanks for letting me wake up today.
There is work to be done. Humor and laughter to pack.
Smiles and hugs to give out that I will give back.

Dear Lord,
Thanks for letting me wake today.
Some days are overwhelming. So much pain I cannot hide.
I take time out with the Lord. Together we cry.

Dear Lord,
Thank you for another day to have weakness and strength.
Thank you for another day to share a piece of you through me.
Thank you for my friends and family.
In the eyes of a stranger, I see you.
In the voice of a child, I hear you.
In my actions, I strive to be you.
Thanks for letting me wake up today.

In my actions, I strive to be you.
Thanks for letting me wake up today.

My storms have been filled with anxiety, depression, abandonment, fear, loneliness, and other uncertainties. After every storm, there has been healing, acceptance, love, laughter and so much more. That's how I survived and conquered. They may always try to take me down but they don't stand a chance.

MY GAME

I played a game with the Devil. I didn't know it was him.
He wore a mask like everyone else and I let him in.
He wore the mask of kindness and he did it extremely well.
The mask was changed for others' eyes yet I could never tell.
I tried to fix the pieces of his broken heart.
Yet for a moment that I looked, the mask was torn apart.
Now everyone can see the Devil in a different way.
What the Devil doesn't know is that it's now my turn to play.
I've played by his rules. I've gone insane.
You fell asleep Devil. This is my game.
Be angry. Shake your fist. Show who you really are.
I will walk away with a smile and a scar.
I sold my soul to the Devil once and in the end I won.
No longer hiding behind my mask, I'm brighter than the sun.
Now remember Devil, if you think it's your turn
You should reconsider cuz you just got burned.

There is something storms do not have that I do—my passions. Storms do not get to choose who I am.

I choose my passion, my life, and my story.

PASSION

You know that thing you love to do?
Do it like your life depends on it...
Because it does.

CHOICES

What do you do when the mad comes to play?
Do you scream at the mad so it will go away?
Do you stomp your feet and beat your hands on the wall?
Do you get on your hands and knees to crawl?
What do you do when the mad wants to creep in?
Do you straighten up and shout with a fist
in the air "You will not win!"
Do you cover your ears then snap at the air, "Not this time!"
Do you curl up in a ball mumbling, "The control is all mine."
Do you take a walk to clear your head or sing a song or two?
Make a list of all the things that you could possibly do.
Do you stop to make a wish with a dandelion flower?
Keep going down the list until the mad has no more power.

EPILOGUE

When it's winter, we wish for summer. When it's summer, we wish for fall. When it's sunny and hot, we wish for rain. When it's raining, we wish for the sun. We sit in the shade or put on sunscreen on sunny days. We use an umbrella when it's raining. We dress in layers during the winter. We learn what to do to protect ourselves the best we can from the different changes. We know we may get sun burnt, wet, or cold, but accept things like that could happen.

While inner storms are similar, we don't always know how to protect ourselves. We wear masks and build walls. Our beliefs, needs, wants, boundaries, and realities change. Sometimes our mental health becomes overloaded at vast speeds, and we begin to question our strength and worth.

Learning to live with chronic pain came with depression, anxiety, pain, and anger. I couldn't protect myself or my family from these storms. That isn't what we had planned.

All I knew is we would get through it together.
But how? Where do we go from here?

A.

B.

C.

ACKNOWLEDGE AND ACCEPT

It is easy to recognize things like being cold, hungry, or tired. We acknowledge and accept them then take action. We may put on a sweater, eat, or sleep. Some things are easier to recognize than others.

Have you ever felt happy, angry, or overwhelmed? Acknowledge whatever you are going through. Accept the feelings for what they are and what you need them for in the moment.

When I wasn't able to drive anymore, I knew that it was best to give up my car and that I wasn't going to get my license renewed. Of course, I wasn't happy about it. I acknowledged and accepted that I had to let go. Telling myself they were just objects and not attaching emotions to them made it easier to accept. I had to grow through the emotions in order to release them.

Accept things are different because change is necessary for growth.

BELIEVE AND BREAKTHROUGH

Take time to listen to your mind, body, and soul. Believe that you are strong and will persevere. Every trial and triumph is a reminder of what you have accomplished and how far you have come. Be thankful every day for what you can do.

Believe that by letting go of things that don't fit anymore then there is space for new things to manifest. Hear, feel, and breathe your power and rhythm. Direct that energy to break through and break free of limiting beliefs, labels, and the masks we wear.

CHALLENGE AND CHOOSE

Challenge yourself to practice breathing with the intention to regain rhythm and calm anxiety. Close your lips and breathe in through your nose. Count to five. Slightly open your lips and breathe out. Count to five. Repeat these steps. With every count, feel where it is coming from. Feel every breath you take as it goes from the chest to the abdomen.

You can practice this not only when anxiety arises but when you're washing dishes, folding laundry, or any task.

Choose what you can do today so that you can say, *I did that. I am choosing something to change my life and my story.* It might be to get out of bed, to get dressed, or to go on a walk even if it's around your house. It might be making a meal, drawing something, or talking to someone in some way whether it be a phone call, text, or in some other way. Whatever you choose, do it for you.

Give yourself credit for all that you do, all that you are, and all that you can be. Follow your heart, take the first step, feel the rhythm, and dance in your purpose.

Mental balance is different for each of us, but we are not alone. We flow into each other's journeys through the beliefs of intuition, higher power, deity, God, or whatever you choose to call it; the fact is we need each other. We can make the world a better place with acceptance, love, understanding, and compassion.

You are loved. You are strong. You make a difference. I believe in you.

Made in the USA
Las Vegas, NV
05 March 2022

45109195R00083